IGGY PECK'S

BIG PROJECT BOOK
FOR AMAZING
ARCHITECTS

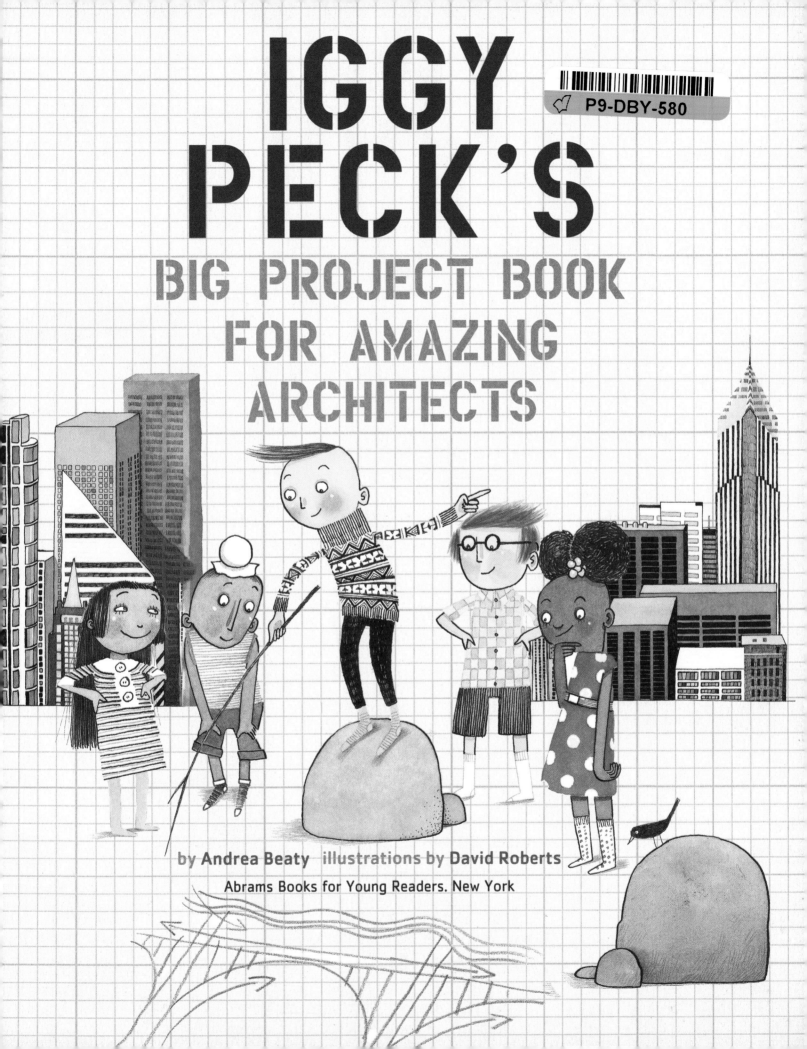

by Andrea Beaty   illustrations by David Roberts

Abrams Books for Young Readers, New York

Architect, architect. What do you see?
I look at a space and see what might be.

Architect, architect. What do you do?
I take an idea and make it come true.

Cataloging-in-Publication Data has been applied for and may be obtained from the Library of Congress.

ISBN 978-1-4197-1892-2

Text copyright © 2017 Andrea Beaty
Illustrations copyright © 2017 David Roberts
Book design by Chad Beckerman and Laura Crescenti

Page 11 (*left*), iStock.com/coward_lion; (*middle left*), iStock.com/Krivinis; (*middle right*), iStock.com/master2; (*right*), iStock.com/TomasSereda. **Page 13** (*top left*), iStock.com/Nattakit; (*top right*), iStock.com/BluePlanetEarth; (*middle*), iStock.com/zoom-zoom. **Page 14**, iStock.com/chameleonseye. **Page 26**, iStock.com/Archipoch. **Page 39**, iStock.com/scanrall. **Page 42**, iStock.com/seb007. **Page 50** (*top left*), iStock.com/goinyk; (*middle*), iStock.com/jremes84; (*bottom*), iStock.com/Kevin_Lucas. **Page 52**, iStock.com/victormaschek. **Page 56** (*bottom*), iStock.com/wingedwolf. **Page 70** (*top left*), iStock.com/zelyanodzevo; (*top right*), iStock.com/princessmaro; (*top middle left*), iStock.com/IrinaKrivoruchko; (*top middle right*), iStock.com/Maria Kats; (*middle left*), iStock.com/rubinat; (*middle*), iStock.com/VectaRay; (*middle right*), iStock.com/Tamirisó; (*bottom left*), iStock.com/L_Kramer; (*bottom right*), iStock.com/lublubachka. **Page 72**, iStock.com/f11photo. **Page 82** (*top left*), iStock.com/Asurobson; (*top middle*), iStock.com/chameleonseye; (*top right*), iStock.com/Tupungato; (*bottom right*), Zaha Hadid Portrait copyright © 2010 Simone Cecchetti, provided under Creative Commons Public License 2.0, flickr.com/photos/eager/16801531300. **Page 83** (*top left*), iStock.com/TomasSereda; (*top middle*), iStock.com/HieronymusUkkel; (*top right*), iStock.com/scaliger; (*bottom left*), William Pereira Photograph courtesy of Special Collections and Archives, UC San Diego; (*bottom middle*), Frank O. Gehry—Parc Des Ateliers copyright © 2010 Andrea Merola, provided under Creative Commons Public License 2.0, flickr.com/photos/eager/4887026398/in/photostream

Printed and bound in U.S.A.
10 9 8 7 6 5 4 3 2 1

Abrams Books for Young Readers are available at special discounts when purchased in quantity for premiums and promotions as well as fundraising or educational use. Special editions can also be created to specification. For details, contact specialsales@abramsbooks.com or the address below.

ABRAMS The Art of Books
115 West 18th Street, New York, NY 10011
abramsbooks.com

World's Greatest Architect

_____

(your picture here)

CONGRATULATIONS!

If you have ever built anything—out of blocks or LEGOs or candy wrappers, you are already an architect . . . just like Iggy Peck! This book is a tool to help you become an even better one. Use the blank spaces for your ideas. Imagine. Draw pictures. Ask questions. Doodle. Create!

Have fun exploring your architectural dreams. You can share your creations with others or keep this doodle book all to yourself. You decide.

This book is for YOU!

THE STORY OF IGGY PECK, ARCHITECT

Iggy Peck has loved architecture since he was just two years old, when he built a great tower using diapers and glue. His mother was amazed until she realized the diapers weren't clean. P.U.!

Little Iggy created architectural wonders from whatever he could find. He built the Great Sphinx of Giza from dirt clods. He built churches and chapels from peaches and apples.

He even built the St. Louis Gateway Arch from pancakes and coconut pie. Iggy studied all kinds of architecture, and he built and built and built . . . until second grade.

Iggy Peck's second grade teacher, Miss Lila Greer, did not love architecture. She once had a terrible experience involving a tall building, a French circus troupe, cheese, and an elevator. Those are all good things by themselves. Together, they were very, very scary.

As a teacher, Miss Lila Greer wanted to keep her students safe from all those things, especially architecture. On the very first day of school, Miss Lila Greer warned her students that there would be "no architecture in here!"

But Iggy was not listening. He was building a chalk castle in the back of the room.

"IGGY PECK!" said Miss Lila Greer, "Stop that right now! Do you need to see the principal?"

"No ma'am," Iggy said.

Iggy's heart sank. He loved learning about architecture most of all. Without it, second grade was a bore.

One day, Iggy's class went on a picnic at Blue River Pass. They crossed a small bridge to a tiny island in the heart of a burbling stream. Iggy was at the end of the line.

As Iggy stepped onto the island—*CRASH! SPLASH!*—the footbridge collapsed into the rushing water. The class was trapped on the island!

"Help!" yelled Miss Lila Greer. "We're trapped! Oh my!"

Miss Lila Greer swayed this way and that way. Her eyeballs rolled back in her head and—*BAM!*—she fainted.

Iggy's classmates were amazed. They did not know what to do. Iggy looked at the rushing water and the far-off shore. He looked at his classmates. He looked at Miss Lila Greer's shoes.

Iggy got an idea!

He drew a blueprint of his idea in the dirt. His classmates pitched in.

When Miss Lila Greer woke up, she saw something amazing. She saw a beautiful bridge stretched across the water.

The bridge was an engineering marvel. It was made of boots, tree roots, fruit leather, string, and even some things one should not mention! (Like the underwear flag at the very top of the bridge!)

As Miss Lila Greer walked over the bridge, she knew that Iggy had a great talent and passion that he needed to share with everyone.

After that day, Iggy taught all the students—and Miss Lila Greer—about architecture because, as Miss Lila Greer realized, "There are worse things to do, when you're in grade two, than to spend your time building a dream."

Iggy collects all kinds of things for his architectural designs.
Here are some things he finds useful. He calls these items his
"ARCHITECT'S TREASURE." You might find them useful, too.

Rubber bands   Paper clips   Toilet paper rolls   Paper towel rolls   Broken toys

Pencils   Glue   Brushes   Ruler   Coffee cans

Ribbon   Scissors   Screws   Tennis balls   Paint

Paper cups   Paper plates   String   Wire   Books

Tape—there are lots of kinds of helpful tape, including: duct tape, packing tape, double-sided tape, Scotch tape, painter's tape, masking tape, and gaffer tape. Each has its own use.

Cardboard and plastic containers from cereal, crackers, cookies, and oatmeal are useful.

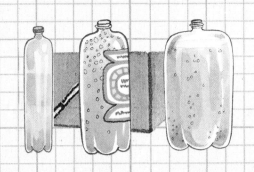

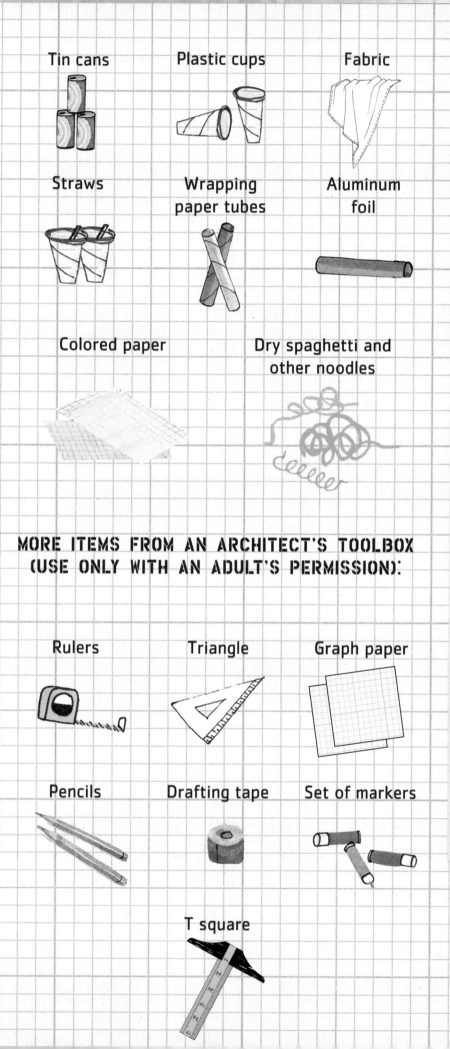

Tin cans

Plastic cups

Fabric

Straws

Wrapping
paper tubes

Aluminum
foil

Colored paper

Dry spaghetti and
other noodles

MORE ITEMS FROM AN ARCHITECT'S TOOLBOX
(USE ONLY WITH AN ADULT'S PERMISSION):

Rulers

Triangle

Graph paper

Pencils

Drafting tape

Set of markers

T square

Where can **you** find
ARCHITECT'S TREASURE?

There are many places you can find
cool things to use in your inventions.

- RECYCLE cardboard boxes, broken
  toys, juice cans, milk jugs, plastic
  lids, and other things your family
  might otherwise throw away. Ask
  permission and make sure they're
  clean and safe to use.

- RUMMAGE SALES and THRIFT
  MARKETS are great places to find
  useful items inexpensively. Finding
  a new use for something old keeps
  it out of the landfill!

- SWAP treasure with your
  architect friends.

- If you can't find a recycled thing
  to use, you might find something
  at a HARDWARE STORE or a
  FABRIC STORE.

AND BE CAREFUL WHEN WORKING
WITH SHARP TOOLS OR BROKEN
PIECES! MAKE SURE AN ADULT IS
ALWAYS NEARBY!

KEEP YOUR ARCHITECT'S TREASURE ORGANIZED!

Treasure is all around. But not everything is a treasure. Choose items that are safe, clean, and useful. A good collection has variety and is well organized.

ORGANIZING YOUR TOOLS AND TREASURE . . .

- keeps them in good shape, so they last longer.

- lets you find what you need when you need it.

- saves money because you don't have to replace things you already have.

- keeps your space clean so you can make things.

- keeps your feet free of holes!

HERE ARE SOME TIPS:

- Decorate and label empty shoeboxes to store under your bed or on a shelf.

- Keep similar things together.

- Small, clean glass jars with lids make great containers for tiny parts like screws and bolts or supplies like rubber bands and string. Clear jars let you easily see what you have!

- A clear plastic shoe holder over the back of a door keeps things organized and easily viewed.

- Hang tools or spools of ribbon on hooks on a pegboard from the hardware store.

- Magnetic strips from the hardware store or sewing store can hold metal scissors or other metal tools.

- An empty can makes a great holder for tools, pencils, and paintbrushes. You can decorate the can, but watch out for sharp edges! Wrap it in decorative paper and ribbon.

Always be safe when you are making something. Protect your eyes with safety glasses.

An architect is always careful!

Don't forget these!

What special things will you add to your Architect's Treasure?

_____

_____

_____

_____

_____

_____

_____

_____

_____

_____

_____

_____

_____

_____

_____

_____

_____

_____

IGGY'S FAVORITE STRUCTURES

1. **The Tower of Pisa** is the campanile, or freestanding bell tower, of the cathedral of the Italian city of Pisa, known worldwide for its unintended tilt.

2. **The Empire State Building** is a 102-story skyscraper located on Fifth Avenue between West 33rd and 34th Streets in Midtown Manhattan, New York City.

3. **St Paul's Cathedral** is an Anglican cathedral. It sits on Ludgate Hill at the highest point of the city of London, England.

4. **The Pyramid of Khufu at Giza** is the largest Egyptian pyramid. It is the only one of the Seven Wonders of the Ancient World still largely intact.

5. **Stonehenge** in Wiltshire, England, is one of the Wonders of the World and the best-known prehistoric monument in Europe.

6. **The Sydney Opera House** is a multivenue performing arts center in Sydney, Australia.

7. **The Colosseum** or **Coliseum**, built of concrete and sand, in Rome, Italy, is the largest amphitheater ever built.

8. **Neuschwanstein Castle** in Bavaria, Germany, was built for King Ludwig II between 1869 and 1886 on a rugged cliff against a scenic mountain backdrop.

9. **The Parthenon** is a former temple on the Athenian Acropolis, Greece, dedicated to the goddess Athena.

Built 1931

102 stories

1250 feet

Built 1868-86

C. 1675-1710

Not so tall

C. 2550-2470 B.C.

C. 2000 BC

C. 72-82 AD

C. 450-424 BC

Built 1957-1973.

10

ABOUT ARCHITECTURE

Architecture makes each place unique. It reflects the history, resources, industries, and environment of the place. It also reflects the lifestyles and personality of the people who live there.

Look carefully at these places. What can you tell about them and the people who live there? What jobs do they do? What is the weather like? What materials are available for them to build their houses?

MAKE YOUR NOTES HERE:

_____

_____

_____

_____

_____

_____

_____

ABOUT ARCHITECTS

Architects take ideas and turn them into structures. They ask lots of questions and use many basic principles in their designs. These are some of the most important principles.

BALANCE · RHYTHM · MOVEMENT · EMPHASIS · CONTRAST · UNITY

BALANCE

Architects use balance to create a feeling of stability. Sometimes they use imbalance to create excitement.

This building is balanced up and down and side to side. It is boring.

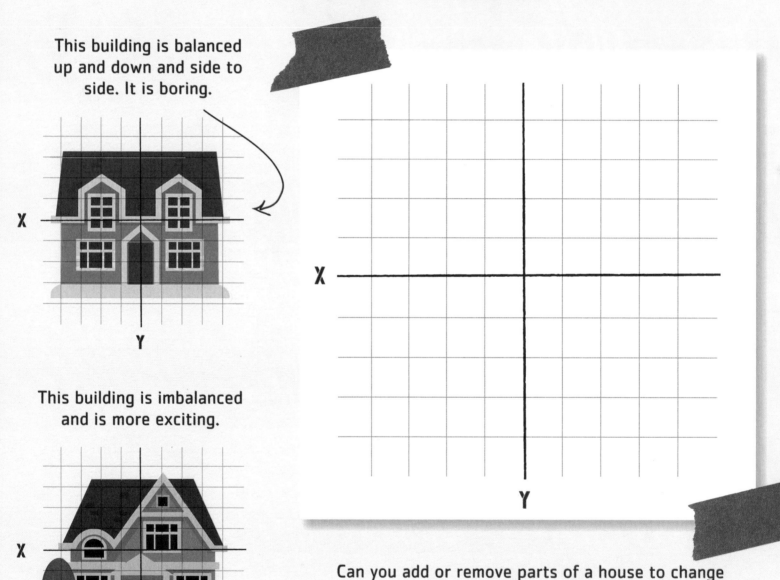

This building is imbalanced and is more exciting.

Can you add or remove parts of a house to change the balance and make it more interesting?

RHYTHM

Buildings, like music, can have parts that form a pattern or rhythm.

The rhythm can be regular like this:

Or this:

Or it could be random like this:

Some dwellings, such as a houseboat, can actually move. Can you design one that also uses lots of curves to add *visual* movement?

MOVEMENT

Most structures with movement don't actually move from one place to another, but they make your eyes want to look from one spot to another, which pulls you toward the building. A pyramid is a great example. Your eye might start looking at the bottom, but pretty soon, your sight will wander up to the top. A design with rhythm can add movement.

EMPHASIS

Sometimes, one part of a building stands out more than the rest. This part has *emphasis*. Like in this case—the minaret of this mosque really stands out.

CONTRAST

Contrast is when one part of a design is very different from the rest. It could be different because of its shape or color, or even its size. The dome of this mosque is a different color from the rest of the building.

Can you design a house with a part that really stands out and is different from the other parts?

UNITY

Unity is using texture, materials, or color in the same way throughout the design.

Think of a building you know that uses the same materials and look all the way across its face (or façade). Is it made of bricks? Stone? Wood?

Can you draw a building that has unity in its design?

ARCHITECT'S WORD SEARCH

Can you find all the words listed to the right in the puzzle below?

(In case you need help, the answer key can be found on page 94.)

```
B T R Q T A P X M A U E I O N J
A G F S G I N D U K R Q T E L E
L A E A U T Y M O C I V B L M E
A P R T L M O V E M E N T U R I
N O K C R T L P T I C A L Q I W
C W Q E H O Z L E M P H A S I S
E E M L A I M H S C A L E P H R
C R U E W K T A I E R W A Y E V
A T E X T U R E N N A O Z A C O
L M Z T P R W V C E O U L G Y D
Y T C R L K D K A T S C H E M I
L P B O Y I O R Z R H Q K O U D
Q C V N A U C L E A R R U Q A M
A R C H I T E C T U R A L E N G
V E U C X G G R E M U M D L M Y
Y U B S P L A N L E C S T Y L E
```

ARCHITECT	UNITY	COLOR	ARCHITECTURAL
BALANCE	SHAPE	LINE	ENGINEER
RHYTHM	FORM	TEXTURE	
EMPHASIS	GOTHIC	BLUEPRINT	
SCALE	ROMANESQUE	PLAN	
MOVEMENT	STYLE	CONTRACTOR	
CONTRAST	ORNAMENTATION	NATURE	

```
R  C  T  T  N  A  T  U  R  E  S  R  I  N  B
C  O  N  T  R  A  C  T  O  R  A  L  S  U  L
O  T  R  O  N  I  C  A  K  T  L  O  L  A  N
L  L  M  C  O  N  T  R  A  S  T  A  C  O  E
O  F  Q  H  K  M  I  A  M  K  C  I  I  R  I
R  C  A  L  I  N  E  Q  U  I  G  T  A  U  U
Q  O  H  R  U  A  L  R  N  R  A  W  P  X  G
O  F  U  U  H  N  F  A  U  T  T  T  U  O  O
T  I  N  A  L  B  H  M  N  F  N  X  K  F  T
C  J  I  P  P  C  H  E  O  I  S  Y  R  T  H
L  I  T  D  E  T  M  S  R  G  I  K  M  A  I
U  P  Y  M  Y  A  J  P  H  J  N  U  J  O  C
W  E  L  H  N  C  E  K  M  Q  E  R  B  G  T
E  E  R  R  E  U  X  D  F  O  R  M  C  E  S
F  N  O  K  L  P  T  H  M  L  V  S  N  Y  Z
I  N  U  B  A  T  E  S  H  A  P  E  D  A  N
```

BUILDING BLUE RIVER CREEK

Architects can help create whole communities. Here's your chance to design and build Iggy's hometown of Blue River Creek using your imagination and your Architect's Treasure. First, follow the instructions on the next few pages to build all the buildings. Then lay out your version of Blue River Creek in any way you like. Think about how you will place the houses. Will they be next to the factories? Rearrange your model and see if other arrangements work better.

HAVE FUN!

HERE ARE SOME TIPS!

- Try to use similar scale for your structures. A tiny factory and a huge house would not work. Imagine if the buildings were in the same town. Guess what? They will be!

- But a town isn't just buildings. Use blue paper or fabric to show bodies of water (rivers, ponds, lakes, oceans).

- Use green paper or fabric to show green spaces like parks, forests, or gardens.

- Create trees from toilet paper or paper towel tubes. Add crinkled tissue paper, cloth, or other items to represent leaves and flowers.

- Use gray paper or fabric to show roadways.

DRAW HERE:

SCHOOL

Iggy Peck, Ada Twist, and Rosie Revere are all students at Blue River Creek Elementary School. What do you think the school looks like? Does it have a library? A playground? How many classrooms? Is it tall? Short? Round? Triangular? Purple and polka-dotted?

Think about your own school. Is there something it needs? You can add it to Blue River Creek Elementary!

Use the space above for your design. Then build a model with your Architect's Treasure. The school will be the start of your model of the entire town!

LIBRARY

Libraries are the heart of a town and show that the town values knowledge and wisdom. Libraries contain bookshelves and places to read, work on computers, hold classes, and meet with friends!

Use this space for your design. Then build a model with your Architect's Treasure. Add the library to your growing model of Blue River Creek!

DRAW HERE:

FACTORIES

What do people make in Blue River Creek? Design one or more factories on this page. Build your model with your Architect's Treasure.

DRAW HERE:

OFFICE BUILDINGS

Some people work in factories, but others work in offices. Can you design an office building to hold all kinds of businesses? What kind of businesses will you include? A monkey-hat company? A cheese-spray company?

DRAW HERE:

DRAW HERE:

SHOPS

The streets of Blue River Creek are filled with interesting shops. Design one here. Build a model of it!

What does your shop sell? Bananas? Candy? Banana-shaped candy? Design the shop building to reflect what the shop sells.

CITY HALL

City Hall is where the mayor and other elected officials meet to create laws for the town. It is also where citizens go to vote, get permits for buildings, and sometimes even go to court!

The City Hall is an important building. Your design should make it stand out!

DRAW HERE:

DRAW HERE:

ZOO

Rosie Revere's uncle is the zookeeper in Blue River Creek. Iggy Peck often visits him with Rosie. Can you design the zoo? How will you keep the snakes and elephants separate? What about the giraffes?

FIRE AND POLICE STATION

Every city needs firefighters and police officers to keep the people safe.
Can you design a combined fire and police station?

DRAW HERE:

OTHER BUILDINGS

What other buildings does Blue River Creek need? Can you design them?
Perhaps you will include a house of worship, a concert hall, a museum?

DRAW HERE:

NOW YOUR TOWN SHOULD BE COMPLETE!

Arrange and rearrange it as much as you like. Draw a picture of the arrangement here.

ALL ABOUT LINES

Architects use lines, color, space, texture, form, shape, and value to create their designs.

Lines go this way and that way—horizontal, vertical, curved, or diagonal.

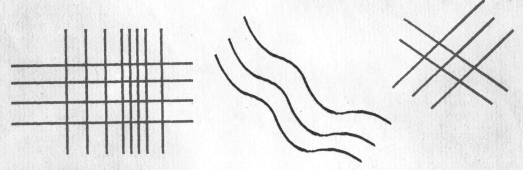

Using only 25 lines, draw an awesome bridge.
No line can be longer than two inches:

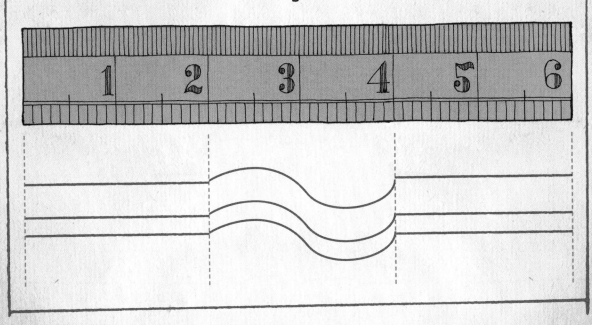

DRAW YOUR 25-LINE BRIDGE HERE:

WHAT DID IGGY BUILD?

One day, Iggy went to the hardware store with his mom.
They needed some grass seed to plant on the Sphinx to keep the dirt clods
from washing away in a big rain. While his mother studied the bags of
grass seed, Iggy wandered off. She found him an hour later.
He had been very, very busy indeed.

"Wow!" the other shoppers
exclaimed.

"Good gracious, Ignatius!"
his mother exclaimed.

"Are you going to pay for that?"
exclaimed the store manager.

Think about the things Iggy would find in a hardware store. Can you draw what he might have built?

ARCHITECTURAL ENGINEERS

Architectural engineers make sure structures are strong and safe.
They understand the engineering challenges involved in architecture and how
to use the materials to make a structure that can hold up to
earthquakes, wind, and other forces.

ARCHITECTURAL ENGINEERING CHALLENGE

Using 20 strands of uncooked spaghetti and 20 miniature marshmallows, build a bridge that spans a 10-inch gap between 2 stacks of books. Test the strength of the bridge by resting a plastic hotel room key or other small plastic card at the center of the bridge. One by one, add pennies. How many will it hold before the bridge collapses? Can you create a better design? How many pennies will it hold?

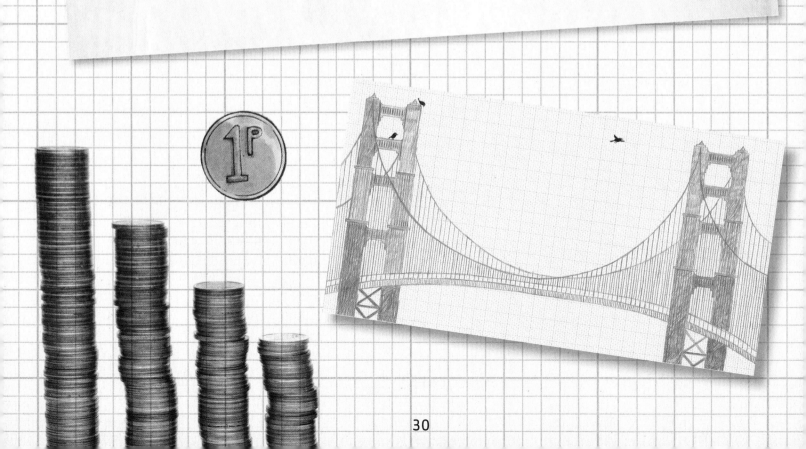

BUILD IT TALL!

Using only 20 plastic straws and 12 inches of masking tape, build the highest stable structure you can!

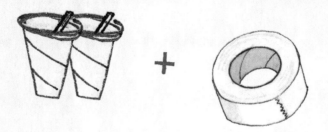

HOW TALL IS IT?

Now, try it with 20 plastic straws and only 5 inches of tape. How tall can you go?

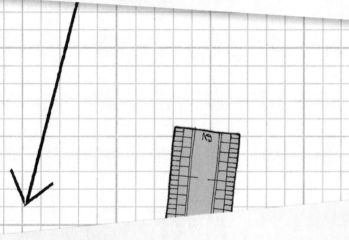

WHAT DID IGGY BUILD?

Iggy was at the grocery store. He was looking for potato chips, but got distracted by all the possible building materials. Can you imagine what he built?

DRAW HERE:

IMAGINE

What if you lived in a swamp with lots of alligators?
The ground is too wet to build upon. Can you design a school in the trees?
Will it be one building or many buildings? How will students and teachers—
but not alligators—get to the classrooms?

Things to include: library, art room, playground, and classrooms.

SENSORY EXPERIMENTS

We experience a place using each of our senses. How it looks is important, but what about how it feels? Are the surfaces smooth? Rough? Uneven? Shiny? We use other senses, too. Add something to this house that will make it smell good. (A flower garden? A perfume fan? A stink removing system?) And add something that will make it *sound* special, too. Wind chimes? A bee hive?

DRAW THEM HERE:

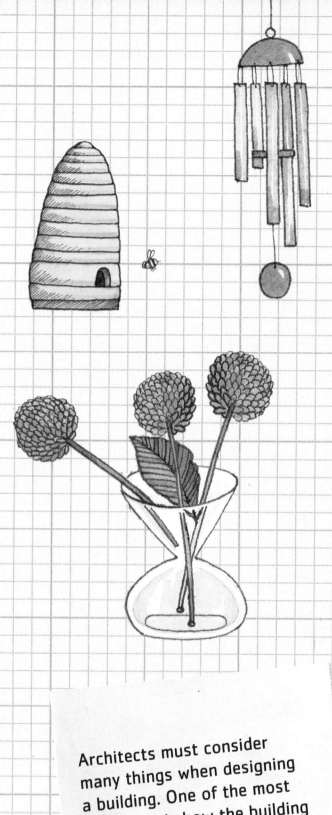

List the things that happen
in your house:

_____

_____

_____

_____

_____

_____

_____

_____

_____

_____

_____

_____

_____

_____

_____

_____

_____

_____

Architects must consider many things when designing a building. One of the most important is how the building will be used. Will it have one use or many?

GOOD LISTENERS

Architects are good listeners. Have a friend or a family member describe what kind of house they would like. Design it for them here:

REVIEW IT!

SHOW the design to your friend or family member. ASK their opinion. Did it fit their requirements? LISTEN to their feedback. ASK QUESTIONS to make sure you understand what they want.

REDESIGN THE HOUSE HERE:

FAVORITE THINGS

Think of your favorite things to do. Can you design a room that lets you do four of them in the same space? Think about clever ways to store items when you aren't using them.

DRAW IT HERE!

 # IMAGINE

Container house: Shipping containers are designed to fit trucks, trains, and cargo ships. Can you design a shipping container house?

DRAW YOUR INTERIOR FLOOR PLAN BELOW:

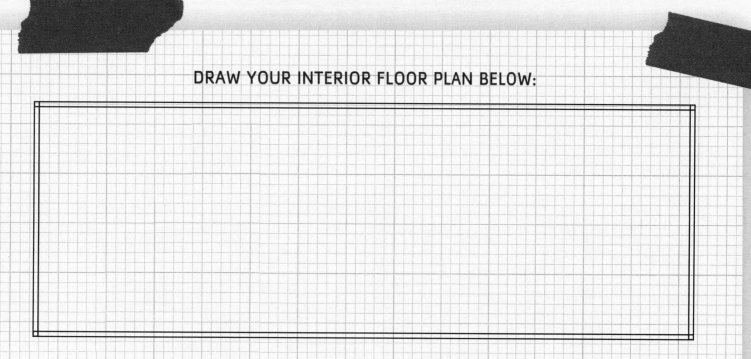

DRAW HOW IT WILL LOOK ON THE OUTSIDE:

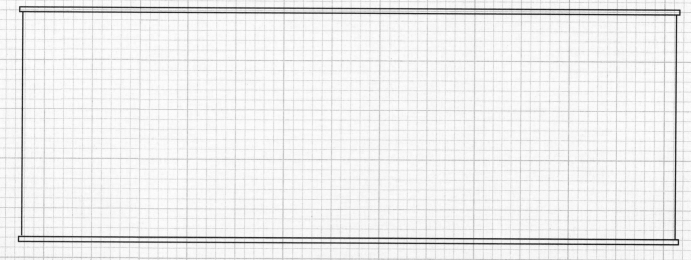

REAL-WORLD PROBLEMS

War, earthquakes, drought, typhoons, and many other man-made and natural catastrophes force people to flee their homes. They must find temporary housing until they can resettle or return to their homes. Nobody knows where or when disaster will strike, so some shelters are made to be light and easy to move and assemble.

Can you design a temporary shelter for a family seeking refuge? It should be mobile, easy to set up, large enough to hold a family, and able to collect water from rain and energy from the sun, wind, or kinetic energy (captured from things that move).

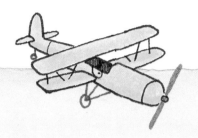

DRAW YOUR DESIGN HERE:

THEY'VE GOT STYLE!

There are many styles of architecture. Styles can develop over many centuries or just a few years. Iggy loves learning about architectural styles. Two of his favorites are Gothic and Romanesque.

Romanesque architecture was a style found in medieval Europe. (It started about the year 1000 AD.) Romanesque architects were copycats. They loved to copy styles from ancient Rome. Especially arches!

Romanesque architecture is full of rounded arches like this:

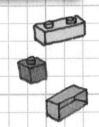

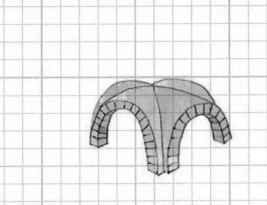

ROMANESQUE architecture is filled with rounded arches. This era's architecture was defined by massive buildings with lots of arches, plus thick walls, pillars, and small windows.

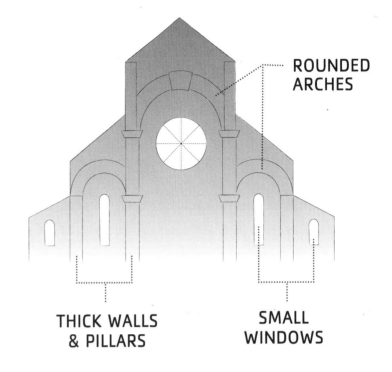

ROUNDED ARCHES

THICK WALLS & PILLARS

SMALL WINDOWS

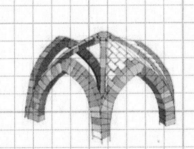

GOTHIC architecture developed later, from the twelfth century to the sixteenth century. Instead of rounded arches, Gothic architecture used pointed arches. The roofs went up, up, up! Architects invented the flying buttress to support the weight of the high walls. They also included large stained glass windows to let in light.

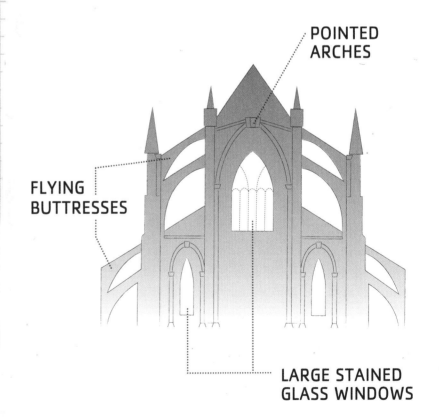

POINTED ARCHES

FLYING BUTTRESSES

LARGE STAINED GLASS WINDOWS

Gothic architecture often included stained glass windows that told stories. Segments of colored glass were held together by bands of lead. Details like facial features were painted onto the glass.

Color these Gothic windows and then create your own design. You can use thick or thin lines to separate segments of color.

I DO NOT LIKE ARCHITECTURE...

Miss Lila Greer did not like architecture until Iggy Peck taught her about it.

Have you ever learned to love something new even though
you did not think you would like it?

DRAW A PICTURE ABOUT IT HERE:

REAL-WORLD PROBLEMS

Climate change is affecting weather patterns around the world.
Widespread droughts increase the frequency of forest fires.

DESIGN A HOME THAT COULD REPEL A FOREST FIRE:

WHAT DID IGGY BUILD?

What could Iggy Peck build with the things in your house?

DRAW IT HERE:

ORNAMENTATION

Many elements of architecture are structural. They determine how a building supports itself. Some are ornamental. They determine how it will look.

Ornamentation changes with architectural eras and styles. Styles might look to nature, history, religion, mythology, art, music, geometry, or other places for inspiration. Create an ornamental design to show what inspires you!

1712–1747:
Bolo Hauz Mosque
in Bukhara

DRAW IT HERE:

**Fourteenth through
seventeenth centuries:**
French Renaissance Bronze
Ornament

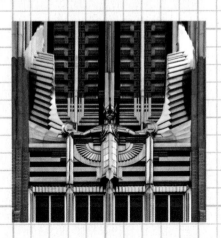

1925–1940:
American Art Deco

GARGOYLES are common ornamentation in Gothic architecture. Gargoyles are creepy or funny statues that sit on the roof or gutter and act as rain spouts.

DRAW A GARGOYLE FOR YOUR HOUSE!

COPYCATS

Buildings can copy other things.
The Sydney Opera House mimics sailboats.

CAN YOU DRAW A HOUSE THAT MIMICS A HAT?

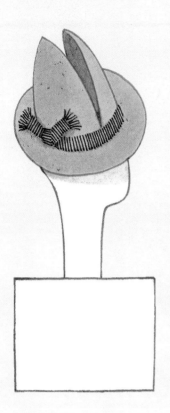

CAN YOU DRAW A HAT THAT MIMICS A HOUSE?

IMAGINE

One day, we will possibly live on Mars.
Can you design a dwelling for Mars? What will you do about air?
Water? Entertainment? Food?

DRAW YOUR DESIGN HERE:

REAL-WORLD PROBLEMS

Water is a limited resource that must be preserved. Design a house that collects water from rain and finds ways to reuse water. The house must be self-sufficient for energy use. Consider using solar, wind, and kinetic energy from the movement of the people who live there.

Draw your design here. The future of our planet rests in your hands!

INSPIRATION IS EVERYWHERE

Look to nature for inspiration. Like many artists, a famous American architect
named Frank Lloyd Wright was inspired by the wide, flat prairie.
It showed in his architecture, which used low, horizontal lines and
natural materials from the prairie, such as stone.

FRANK LLOYD WRIGHT
American architect
1867–1959

Think of a place in nature that you love. A forest? A lake? Can this place inspire you? Draw your ideas here.

ARE YOU A MIND READER?

Probably not. Neither are contractors or builders. They need very precise directions from the architect. Without great directions, they will build something different than what the architect imagined.

WITH A FRIEND: Draw a small house. Do not show it to your friend. Instead, use words to describe your house, and have your friend use a separate piece of paper to draw what you have described. Does it look like the house you drew?

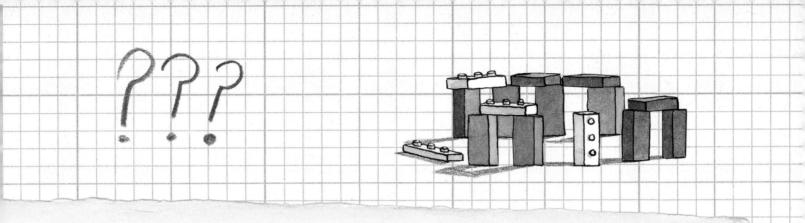

SWAP TURNS and see if you can draw the house your friend describes.

MAKE A PLAN

Architectural plans used to be called **BLUEPRINTS** because of the special paper that architects used to create and copy them. Architectural plans use symbols to represent the parts of the building. The symbols are important in communicating to contractors and builders—and to building owners—precisely how the structure will come together.

HERE ARE SOME OF THEM:

Wall

Window

Doorway

Hinged door

Stairs

Curved stairs

Bathtub

Freestanding sink

Toilet

Shower

Cabinet with sink

Stove

Fridge

Cabinet

Washer

Dryer

Use the symbols to create a simple home plan.

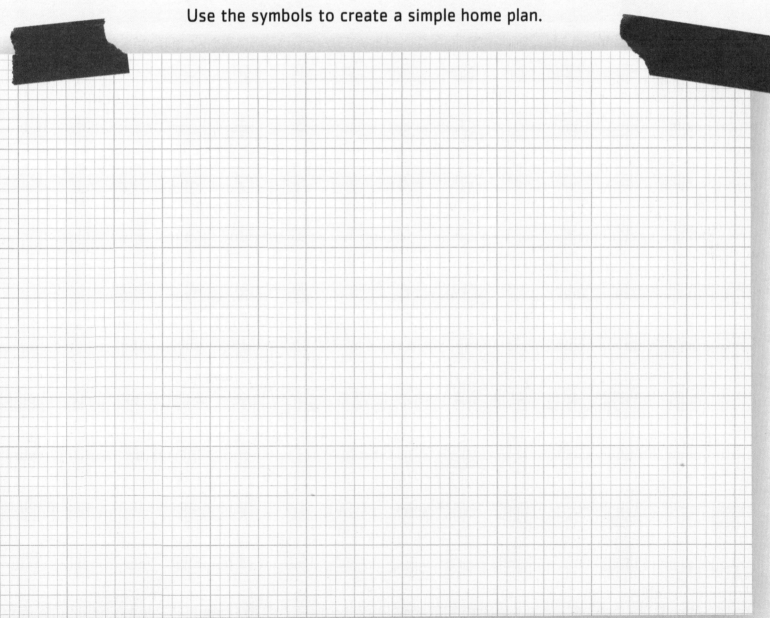

STUFF GOES INTO HOUSES!

Houses and buildings almost always contain furniture (tables, sofas, beds) and fixtures (sinks, toilets, tubs). Architects must consider these items when designing spaces. A bathroom that's too tiny for a toilet wouldn't be very useful!

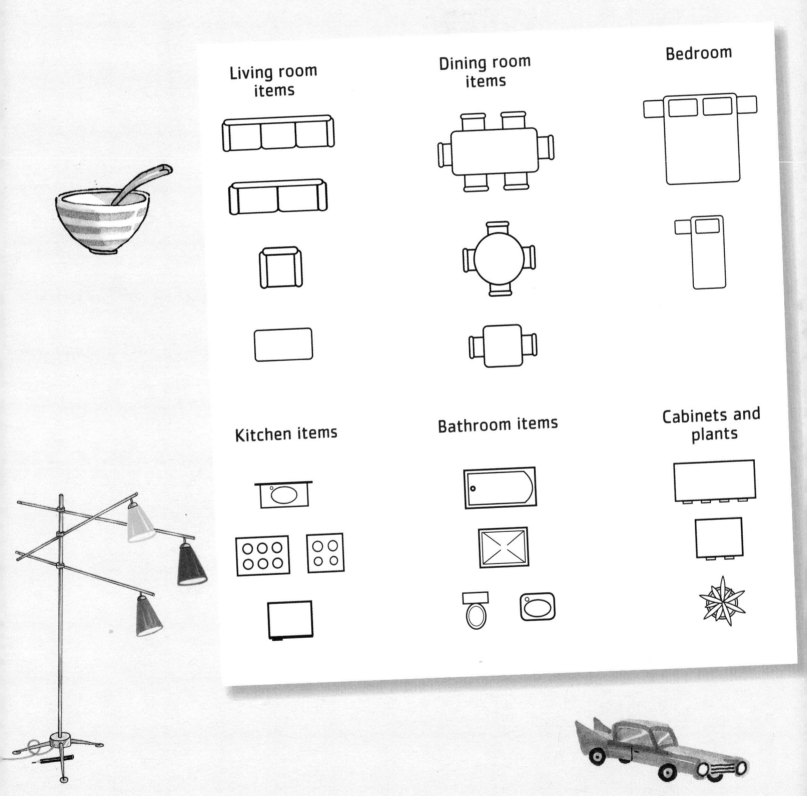

Living room items

Dining room items

Bedroom

Kitchen items

Bathroom items

Cabinets and plants

How would you arrange the furniture and fixtures for this home?

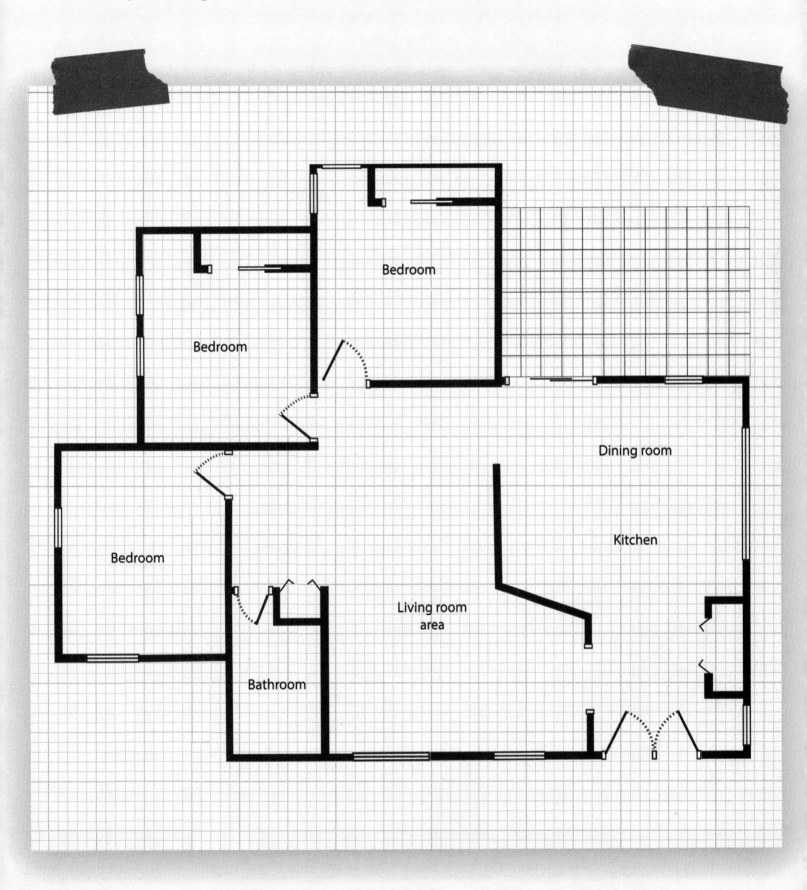

MISS LILA GREER'S HOME AWAY FROM SCHOOL

Miss Lila Greer bought this tiny house but she wants to expand it. She needs a library for her new architecture, science, and engineering books. Can you expand her house? What other rooms would you add?

The plan of her current house is shown below. The black sections are load-bearing walls that help hold up the house and cannot be changed. Other walls and features (in blue) can be easily removed.

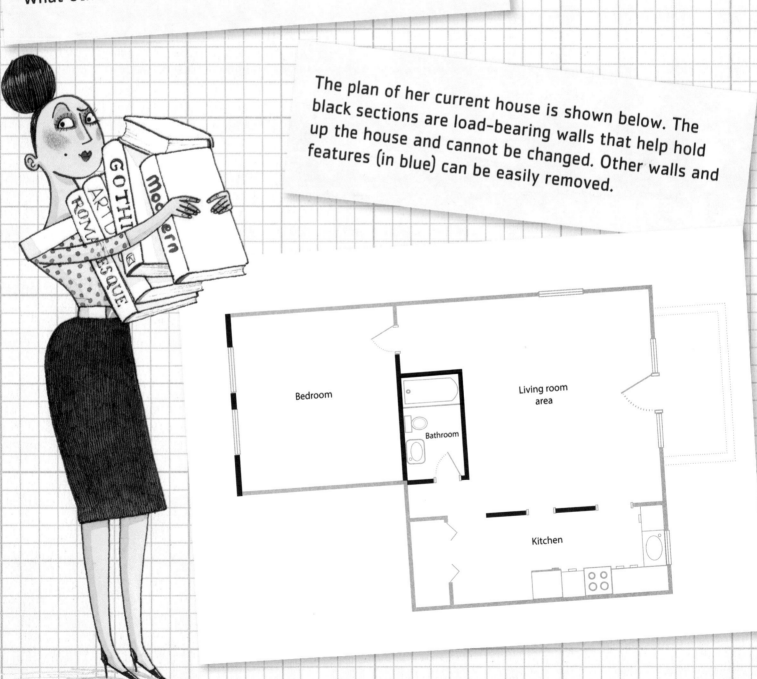

Bedroom

Bathroom

Living room area

Kitchen

How will you change the house?

65

USE WHAT YOU'VE GOT

People have always used what's handy and abundant to create structures:

Stone   Timber   Grass

Mud   Snow

Iggy sometimes builds just with fruit he finds in the fridge!

What if you live in a place where candy is the most abundant resource? What kind of house would you build? Draw it here.

DETAILS!

These windows and doors show different architectural styles.

Some window styles:

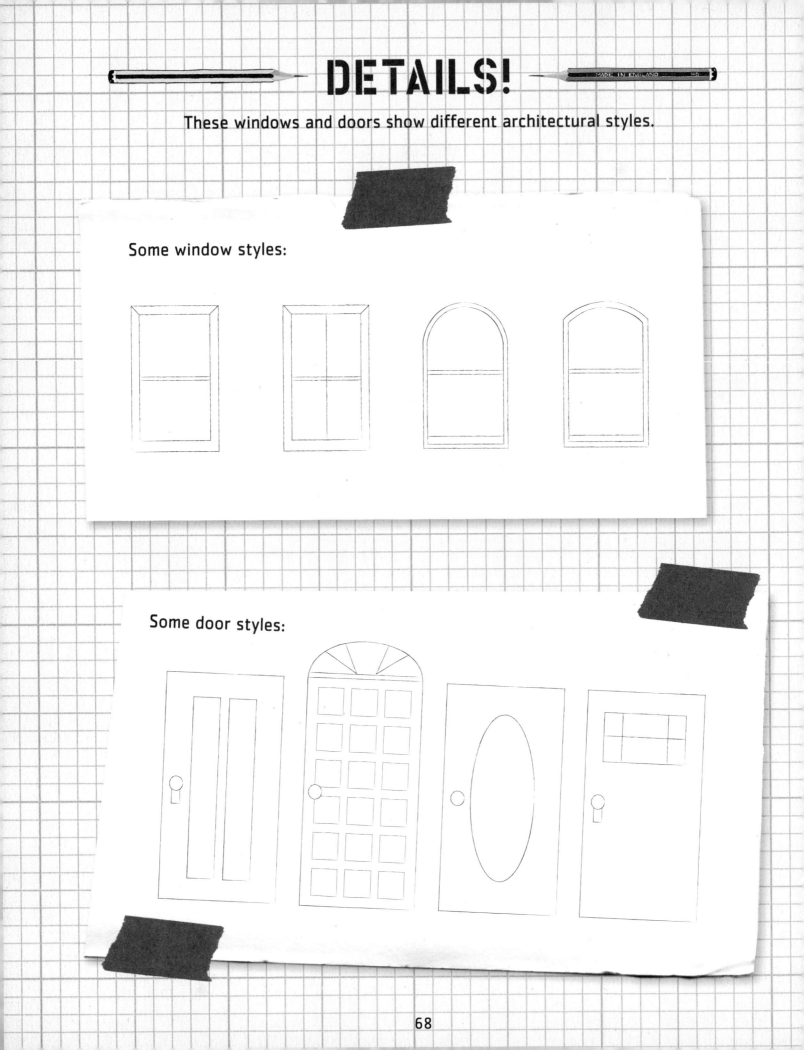

Some door styles:

Design your own style of windows and doors.
Add them to a simple façade and see how it looks.

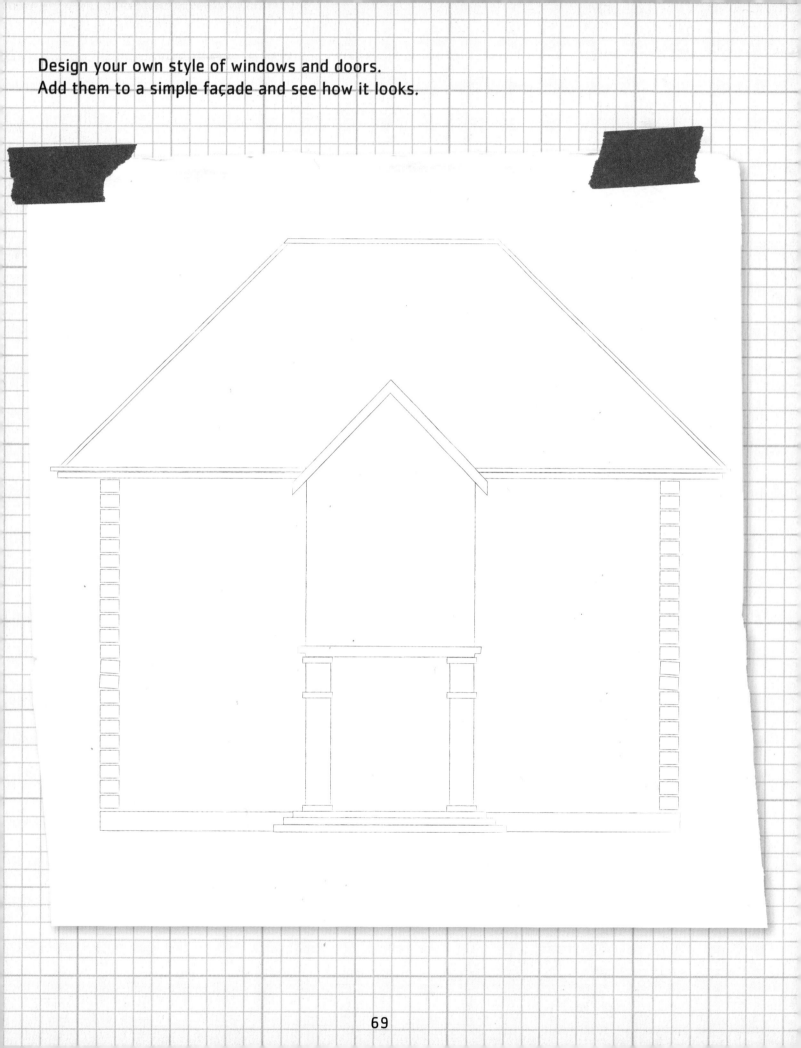

SIMPLE OR FANCY?
YOU DECIDE

Each era of architecture has its own style.
The ornamentation of windows, doors, ceilings, eaves, and other
building features play a big role in that.

HERE ARE SOME EXAMPLES:

HINDU

ROCOCO

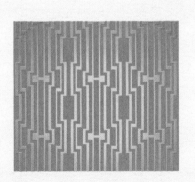

ART DECO

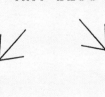

Create your own ornamentation here:

How would you add it to
this simple door?

WHAT'S MISSING?

Sometimes, what's missing in a design is the most interesting part.
The St. Louis Gateway Arch is 630 feet tall and 630 feet from foot to foot,
but the biggest part of it is the hole in the middle.

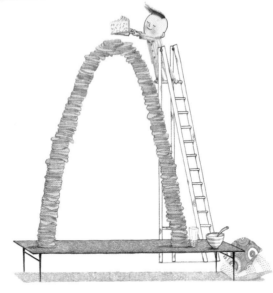

Design a tower that uses empty space to add interest.

LOCATION, LOCATION, LOCATION

Not every house is built on bare, flat land.
What kind of house would you create for this setting?

Think about the sun, wind, and water. Consider the view from different angles. How will you get to the house? Boat? Car? Cheese-copter? Ladder? Submarine?

BOUNCY HOUSE

On the Planet of Rubber Balls, the only resource for building a house is—yep! you guessed it!—rubber balls.

CREATE a house from rubber balls. Use balls of different colors and sizes to make it interesting. How will you keep the house from bouncing away?

WHAT DID IGGY BUILD?

The Blue River Creek Zoo is remodeling the South American exhibit.
While that's happening, the mammals must live with other animals. The sloths are
rooming with the giraffes. It's not working out. Can you design a temporary
structure that lets sloths and giraffes live together happily?

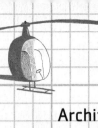

HEAD IN THE CLOUDS

Architecture evolves with the invention of new materials. Imagine a future
building made from lighter-than-air floating bricks. Design a house that floats above
the ground. Include a way to get into the house from the ground.

HAUNTED HOUSE

An architect considers the personality, needs, and abilities of the inhabitants when designing a house. Could you design a haunted house?

DRAW IT HERE:

ENVIRONMENTALLY FRIENDLY HOUSES

The planet's resources are limited. Energy use is a vital consideration in architecture. Can you design an environmentally friendly house using these energy-saving supplies?

Solar tiles

Wind turbines

Think about renewable energy sources such as solar power, wind, and kinetic energy. Where will water come from, and how will it be used? What about recycling?

Energy-efficient glass

Roof gardens

DRAW YOUR HOUSE HERE:

BUILDING MATCH GAME

Can you match each iconic work of architecture with its architect?
(Answers are on p. 94.)

Heydar Aliyev Center	Transamerica Pyramid	Walt Disney Concert Hall
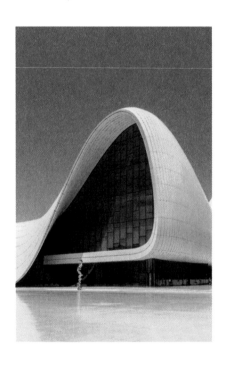		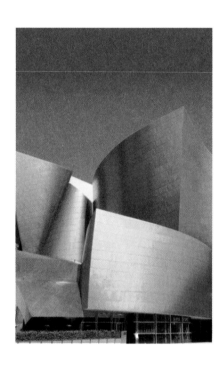

A = Antoni Gaudí
Spain
1852–1926

B = Gustave Eiffel
France
1832–1923

C = Zaha Hadid
United Kingdom
1950–2016

Sagrada Família	Elizabeth Tower (Big Ben)	Eiffel Tower

D = William Pereira United States 1909–1985	**E = Frank Gehry** United States b. 1929	**F = Augustus Pugin** United Kingdom 1812–1852

IMAGINE

DESIGN AN UNDERWATER HOUSE: How will you get there from the surface of the ocean? How will it withstand the pressure of the ocean? How will you see around in such a dark place? What energy sources will it use? How will you keep giant squids from latching onto the house?

WHAT DID IGGY BUILD?

Iggy is at the beach. He is impressed with all the sand castles
and thinks he can build something even more ambitious.
Can you imagine what he built?

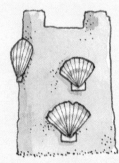

LOCATION, LOCATION, LOCATION

What kind of houses would you create to fit in this crowded setting?

DRAW YOUR HOUSE HERE:

THINKING ABOUT OTHERS

Each person has his or her own needs for a home. Consider a person who uses a wheelchair. Walk through your house and list the improvements that would help a person in a wheelchair get into the house, get around inside the house, cook, bathe, relax, sleep, and play.

LIST YOUR IMPROVEMENTS HERE:

_____

_____

_____

_____

_____

_____

_____

_____

_____

_____

DRAW YOUR REDESIGN HERE:

How could you modify your house for a person who was blind? Close your eyes and see if you can navigate your house easily. What could you redesign to help?

MAKE YOUR MARK

Professional architects use special stamps to identify their work.

Iggy has his own stamp of approval. Can you create your own stamp?

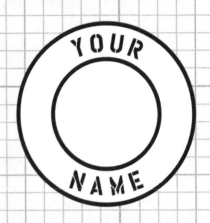

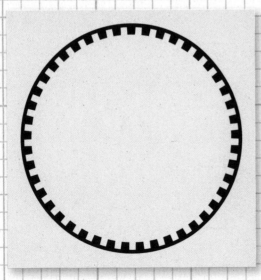

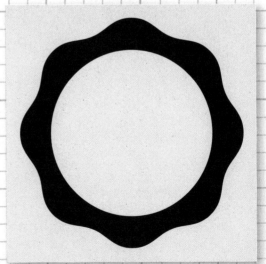

YOU'RE AN ARCHITECT!

LIST YOUR BIG PLANS HERE:

_____

_____

_____

_____

_____

_____

_____

_____

_____

Now start drawing your dreams:

ANSWER KEY

From pp.16–17:

```
B T R Q T A P X M A U E I O N J R Z R C T T N A T U R E S R I N B
A G F S G I N D U K R Q T E L E N S C O N T R A C T O R A L S U L
L A E A U T Y M O C I V B L M E C H O T R O N I C A K T L O L A N
A P R T L M O V E M E N T U R I N G L L M C O N T R A S T A C O E
N O K C R T L P T I C A L Q I W J Y O F Q H K M I A M K C I R I I
C W Q E H O Z L E M P H A S I S K E R C A L I N E Q U I G T A U U
E E M L A I M H S C A L E P H R A L Q O H R U A L R N R A W P X G
  C R U E W K T A I E R W A Y E V I M O F U U H N F A U T T U O T
A T E X T U R E N N A O Z A C O U S T I N A L B H M N F N X K F T
L M Z T P R W V C E O U L G Y D K M C J I P P C H E O I S Y R T H
Y T C R L K D K A T S C H E M I C A L I T D E T M S R G I K M A I
L P B O Y I O R Z R H Q K O U D K J U P Y M Y A J P H J N U J O C
Q C V N A U C L E A R R U Q A M W K W E L H N C E K M Q E R B G T
A R C H I T E C T U R A L E N G I N E E R R E U X D F O R M C E S
V E U C X G G R E M U M D L M Y D B F N O K L P T H M L V S N Y Z
Y U B S P L A N L E C S T Y L E A R I N U B A T E S H A P E D A N
```

From pp. 82–83:

Heydar Aliyev Center	Transamerica Pyramid	Walt Disney Concert Hall	Sagrada Família	Elizabeth Tower (Big Ben)	Eiffel Tower
C = Zaha Hadid	D = William Pereira	E = Frank Gehry	A = Antoni Gaudí	F = Augustus Pugin	B = Gustave Eiffel